The Childhood Memories
of

_____

Date

Published in Nashville, Tennessee, by Tommy Nelson®, a Division of Thomas Nelson, Inc.

Designed by Koechel Peterson & Associates, Inc.

Unless otherwise indicated, Scripture quotations are from the INTERNATIONAL CHILDREN'S BIBLE,
NEW CENTURY VERSION®, copyright © 1986, 1988, 1999 by Tommy Nelson®,
a Division of Thomas Nelson, Inc., Nashville, Tennessee. Used by permission.

Scripture quotations marked (NKJV) are from the NEW KING JAMES VERSION,
copyright © 1982 by Thomas Nelson, Inc. Used by permission. All rights reserved.

ISBN 0-8499-7783-5

03 04 05 06 07 QW 5 4 3 2 1

A KEEPSAKE JOURNAL

My Childhood Memories

Featuring the art of
THOMAS KINKADE

Written by Tama Fortner

www.tommynelson.com
A Division of Thomas Nelson, Inc.
www.ThomasNelson.com

I REMEMBER . . .
  picnics in the park
  and chasing lightning bugs after dark.
I remember . . .
  games of catch
  and teaching the new puppy to fetch.
I remember . . .
  birthday cakes
  and splashing trips to the lake.
I remember . . .
  kisses goodnight
  and hugs that hold me tight.
I remember . . .
  prayers lifted to the Lord above
  and hearts brimming over with love.

I remember so many things.
Thank you, God, for all my rememberings.

TAMA FORTNER

Family is important. Write a message about how much your family means to you below.

Dear _____,

_____
_____
_____
_____
_____
_____
_____
_____
_____
_____
_____
_____
_____
_____
_____
_____
_____
_____
_____
_____
_____

Love,

_____

All About Me!

My full name is _____

_____

My birth date is _____. I am _____ years old.

I am most like my mom in the way I

_____

_____

_____

I am most like my dad in the way I

_____

_____

_____

But I am different from my mom and dad in the way I

_____

_____

_____

*"Before you were born,
I set you apart for a special work."*

JEREMIAH 1:5

The thing I like most about myself

_____

_____

_____

Something I would like to change about myself

_____

_____

Home Is Where My Heart Is

My hometown is

My home is like

The best thing about our home

My room

Mom makes our home special by

I will live in the house of the Lord forever.

Psalm 23:6

Dad makes our home special by

_____

_____

_____

_____

My Mom and Me

My mother's name is _____,

but I call her _____.

A special thing about my mom

_____

_____

_____

_____

The first memory I have of my mom

_____

_____

_____

_____

_____

_____

The most wonderful thing my mom ever said to me

_____

_____

_____

_____

_____

When I was sad or frightened, my mom made me feel better by

_____

_____

_____

_____

_____

"What *do* girls do who haven't any mothers
to help them through their troubles?"

LOUISA MAY ALCOTT
Little Women

My Mom Teaches Me

My mom teaches me about God by

She teaches me how to love by

I hope that one day my mom will teach me how to

My mom is the best at

I remember your true faith.
That kind of faith first belonged to
your grandmother Lois and to your mother Eunice.

2 TIMOTHY 1:5

The thing I love most about my mom

Dear Mom . . .

Write a letter to your mom telling her all that she means to you.

She opens her mouth with wisdom,
And on her tongue is the law of kindness.

PROVERBS 31:26 (NKJV)

My Dad and Me

My father's name is _____ ,

but I call him _____ .

A special thing about my dad

_____

_____

_____

_____

_____

The first memory I have of my dad

The most wonderful thing my dad ever said to me

When I was sad or frightened, my dad made me feel better by

"It's not easy to learn to whistle
if there's no one to show you how."

JANUSZ KORCZAK
King Matt the First

My Dad Teaches Me

My dad teaches me about God by

_____

_____

_____

_____

He teaches me how to love by

_____

_____

_____

_____

I hope that one day my dad will teach me how to

_____

_____

_____

My dad is the best at

_____

_____

_____

_____

If you go the wrong way—to the right or to the left—
you will hear a voice behind you. It will say,
"This is the right way. You should go this way."

Isaiah 30:21

The thing I love most about my dad

Dear Dad . . .

Write a letter to your dad telling him all that he means to you.

The righteous man walks in his integrity;
His children are blessed after him.

PROVERBS 20:7 (NKJV)

My Brothers and Sisters

I have _____ brothers and _____ sisters.

Their names and ages are

_____

_____

The things I like best about them are

_____

_____

_____

Together, we like to

_____

_____

_____

My favorite thing for our family to do

_____

_____

_____

"You must love each other as I have loved you."

JOHN 13:34

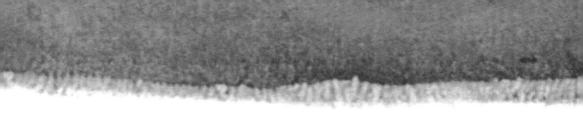

I will always remember when we

My Grandparents (Dad's Mom and Dad)

My grandmother's name is _____ ,
but I call her _____ .

My grandfather's name is _____ ,
but I call him _____ .

The thing I love most about my grandmother

_____

_____

_____

The thing I love most about my grandfather

_____

_____

_____

Visiting my grandparents is special to me because

_____
_____
_____
_____
_____

My favorite memory of my grandparents

_____
_____
_____
_____
_____

A family tradition I look forward to at my grandparents' house

_____
_____
_____
_____

Beloved, let us love one another, for love is of God;
and everyone who loves is born of God and knows God.

1 JOHN 4:7 (NKJV)

My Grandparents (Mom's Mom and Dad)

My grandmother's name is _____ ,
but I call her _____ .

My grandfather's name is _____ ,
but I call him _____ .

The thing I love most about my grandmother

_____
_____
_____
_____

The thing I love most about my grandfather

_____
_____
_____
_____

Visiting my grandparents is special to me because

_____
_____
_____
_____
_____

For whatever things were written before
were written for our learning, that we through the patience
and comfort of the Scriptures might have hope.

ROMANS 15:4 (NKJV)

My favorite memory of my grandparents

A family tradition I look forward to at my grandparents' house

Surrounded by Love

Place photos of family members around your picture.
Nearby, write each person's name and relationship to you.

Attach photo here.

Attach photo here.

Attach a photo of you here.

Attach photo here.

Attach photo here.

Attach photo here.

Attach photo here.

How many *other* members of your family can you name?

Attach photo here.

Attach photo here.

Attach photo here.

My Prayers to God

For my family, I pray that

_____

_____

_____

_____

For my friends, I pray that

_____

_____

_____

_____

For the world, I pray that

_____

_____

_____

_____

For myself, I pray that

_____

_____

_____

_____

_____

The Lord listens when I pray to him.

PSALM 4:3

Other things I pray about

_____

_____

_____

_____

_____

Sometimes, I Wonder . . .

Why is the sky blue? Where is heaven?
Why did God make spiders and snakes?

Write down some of the things you wonder about.

_____

_____

_____

_____

_____

_____

_____

_____

_____

_____

_____

_____

_____

_____

_____

_____

Do you know how God controls the clouds
and makes his lightning flash?
Do you know how the clouds hang in the sky?
They are the miracles of God, who knows everything.

JOB 37:15–16

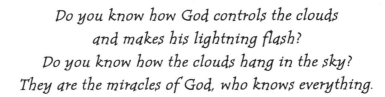

God Is Good

I believe God is

_____

_____

_____

_____

My image of God is

_____

_____

_____

_____

I first knew God was real when

_____

_____

_____

_____

Heaven is

_____

_____

_____

_____

We know that in everything
God works for the good of those who love him.

ROMANS 8:28

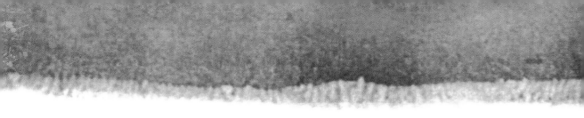

I believe that angels

God Is Great

My favorite Bible story

_____

_____

_____

_____

_____

I like this story because

_____

_____

_____

_____

My favorite Bible verse

_____

_____

_____

_____

To me, this verse means

_____

_____

_____

_____

_____

_____

*Blessed are the pure in heart,
For they shall see God.*

MATTHEW 5:8 (NKJV)

When I get to heaven, the first thing I am going to ask God

Hopes, Dreams, Wishes

Someday I want to

Sometimes I even dream of being

I've always wished that I could

And I just can't wait until

_____

_____

_____

I like to imagine I am

_____

_____

_____

When I was younger, I used to pretend

_____

_____

_____

I hope to be the kind of person who

_____

_____

_____

May he give you what you want.
May all your plans succeed.

PSALM 20:4

Growing Up Is Hard to Do

I was embarrassed when

_____

_____

_____

One of the hardest things for me

_____

_____

_____

Ways Mom helped me

_____

_____

_____

Ways Dad helped me

_____

_____

_____

Be kind and loving to each other.
Forgive each other just as God forgave you in Christ.

EPHESIANS 4:32

Ways my friends helped me

_____

_____

_____

I could help someone younger by

_____

_____

_____

_____

Hurray! . . . Um . . . Oops?

When I do something really terrific, I love it when my mom

_____

_____

_____

_____

When I do something really terrific, I love it when my dad

_____

_____

_____

_____

My mom loves me, even when I

_____

_____

_____

_____

My dad loves me, even when I

_____

_____

_____

_____

Love is patient and kind.

1 CORINTHIANS 13:4

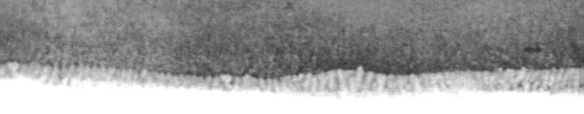

When I'm a parent, I will always

_____

_____

_____

_____

Friends Are Forever

My best friend is _____ , because _____
_____
_____
_____

The friend who makes me laugh is _____ ,
because _____
_____
_____
_____

The friend I've had the longest is _____ .
We like to _____
_____
_____
_____

Attach a photo
or drawing of you
with your friend(s)

Thank you for my friend next door,
And my friend across the street,
And please help me to be a friend
To everyone I meet.

ANONYMOUS

Just for Laughs

Things that make me smile

Things that make me laugh out loud

Our funniest moment as a family

_____
_____
_____
_____

A funny thing Mom did

_____
_____
_____

A funny thing Dad did

_____
_____
_____
_____

A funny thing I did

_____
_____
_____
_____

I never saw a Purple Cow;
I never hope to see one;
But I can tell you, anyhow,
I'd rather see than be one.

GELETT BURGESS
The Burgess Nonsense Book

The Things I Like Best

My favorite rhyme or poem

My favorite thing to do

My favorite television show

My favorite day of the week is _____, because

My favorite time of the year is _____, because

The world is so full of a number of things,
I'm sure we should all be as happy as kings.
ROBERT LOUIS STEVENSON

Thank You, God, For . . .

Make a list of all the things you are thankful for. They can be little things or big things—from a night with no homework to your mom and dad.

It is good to praise the Lord,
to sing praises to God Most High.

Psalm 92:1

Snips, Snails, Puppy Dog Tails

My very first pet

I always wanted

Animals that followed me home

The funniest thing my pet ever did

Dear Father,
Hear and bless
Thy beasts and singing birds.
And guard with tenderness
Small things that have no words.

UNKNOWN

My favorite book about an animal

My favorite animal movie

Teddy Bears, Teapots, Trains

The first toy I remember playing with

_____

_____

_____

When I was sad or scared, I always wanted my

_____

_____

_____

A grown-up toy I'd like to have

_____

_____

_____

_____

When I was younger, I collected

_____

_____

_____

_____

Now my favorite thing to collect is

_____

_____

_____

_____

The best thing about my collection is

_____

_____

_____

_____

_____

"Do not lay up for yourselves treasures on earth . . .
but lay up for yourselves treasures in heaven."

MATTHEW 6:19, 20 (NKJV)

Making Music

My favorite kind of music

My favorite song when I was younger

My favorite song now

The song I most like to sing

My favorite Christian music

The band I like most

The musician I like most

Sing psalms, hymns, and spiritual songs
with thankfulness in your hearts to God.

Colossians 3:16

The musical instrument(s) I like best

_____

_____

The musical instrument I play or would like to play is a
_____ , because _____

_____

_____

Artist at Work

To me, art is

The type of art I like best (paintings, sculptures, photography)

An artist whose work I admire

My earliest creations were

These days, I like to create using

_____

_____

Other arts or crafts that I enjoy

_____

_____

"The best way to know God is to love many things."
VINCENT van GOGH

Books, Wonderful Books!

The first book I remember Mom reading to me

_____

_____

The first book I remember Dad reading to me

_____

_____

The first book I remember reading all by myself

_____

_____

My favorite book

_____

_____

If I were to write a book, it would be about

_____

_____

_____

_____

_____

_____

What is the use of a book, thought Alice,
without pictures or conversations?
LEWIS CARROLL
Alice's Adventures in Wonderland

The Writer in Me

Write a story about a fun day you and your family shared.

Trust in the LORD with all your heart, . . .
And He shall direct your paths.

PROVERBS 3:5–6 (NKJV)

Food, Food, Food!

My all-time favorite foods

My favorite snacks

My favorite flavor of ice cream

If I could, I would eat as much as I want of

My mom is the best at cooking

My dad is the best at cooking

Animal crackers, and cocoa to drink,
That is the finest of suppers, I think;
When I'm grown up and can have what I please
I think I shall always insist upon these.

CHRISTOPHER MORLEY
Chimneysmoke

My favorite family meal(s)

_____

_____

_____

Our family's favorite restaurant(s)

_____

_____

_____

At the Movies

The first movie I remember seeing at a movie theater

The very best movie I ever saw

My favorite video or DVD

The best cartoon

One movie I wish I had never seen

If I were to make a movie, it would be about

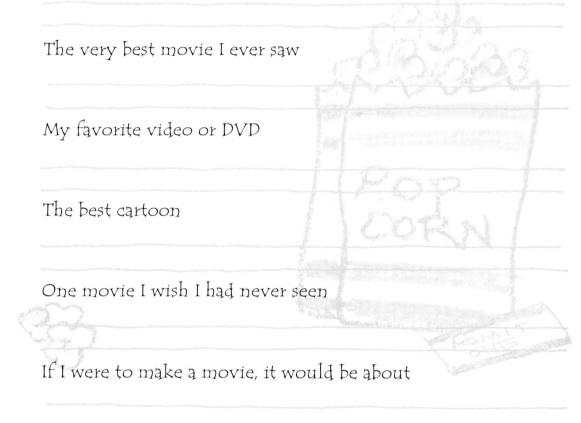

"No person who is enthusiastic about his work
has anything to fear from life."
SAMUEL GOLDWYN

The Games We Play

Some games my family plays together

_____
_____
_____
_____

My favorite outdoor game

_____
_____
_____
_____

The best board game

_____
_____
_____
_____

My favorite video and computer games

_____
_____
_____
_____

Let all that you do be done with love.

1 Corinthians 16:14 (NKJV)

I'm best at playing

Off We Go!

The best family trip I ever took

_____
_____
_____

The most adventurous family trip I've taken

_____
_____
_____

The farthest I have gone from home with my family

_____
_____
_____

The place I would most like to see is _____ ,
because _____
_____

My favorite place to go when it is just Mom and me

_____

_____

My favorite place to go when it is just Dad and me

_____

_____

Attach
photographs of
family trips

The Lord will guard you as you come and go,
both now and forever.

PSALM 121:8

My Big Adventures

The biggest adventure I've ever had

One day, I am going to

My favorite place to go exploring

The best place for a hideout

"The LORD your God is with you wherever you go."

JOSHUA 1:9 (NKJV)

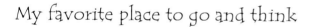

My favorite place to go and think

_____

_____

When I'm there, I like to think about

_____

_____

_____

_____

School Days

The name of my school is ⎯⎯⎯⎯⎯⎯⎯⎯⎯⎯ .

My favorite teacher is ⎯⎯⎯⎯⎯⎯⎯⎯⎯⎯ .

The subject I like to study most is ⎯⎯⎯⎯⎯⎯⎯⎯ .

I think school ⎯⎯⎯⎯⎯⎯⎯⎯⎯⎯⎯⎯⎯⎯⎯⎯⎯

⎯⎯⎯⎯⎯⎯⎯⎯⎯⎯⎯⎯⎯⎯⎯⎯⎯⎯⎯⎯⎯⎯⎯

My favorite part about school ⎯⎯⎯⎯⎯⎯⎯⎯⎯

⎯⎯⎯⎯⎯⎯⎯⎯⎯⎯⎯⎯⎯⎯⎯⎯⎯⎯⎯⎯⎯⎯⎯

⎯⎯⎯⎯⎯⎯⎯⎯⎯⎯⎯⎯⎯⎯⎯⎯⎯⎯⎯⎯⎯⎯⎯

Mom helps me with my homework by ⎯⎯⎯⎯⎯⎯

⎯⎯⎯⎯⎯⎯⎯⎯⎯⎯⎯⎯⎯⎯⎯⎯⎯⎯⎯⎯⎯⎯⎯

⎯⎯⎯⎯⎯⎯⎯⎯⎯⎯⎯⎯⎯⎯⎯⎯⎯⎯⎯⎯⎯⎯⎯

Dad helps me with my homework by ⎯⎯⎯⎯⎯⎯

⎯⎯⎯⎯⎯⎯⎯⎯⎯⎯⎯⎯⎯⎯⎯⎯⎯⎯⎯⎯⎯⎯⎯

⎯⎯⎯⎯⎯⎯⎯⎯⎯⎯⎯⎯⎯⎯⎯⎯⎯⎯⎯⎯⎯⎯⎯

⎯⎯⎯⎯⎯⎯⎯⎯⎯⎯⎯⎯⎯⎯⎯⎯⎯⎯⎯⎯⎯⎯⎯

"I am the Lord your God.
I teach you to do what is good."

Isaiah 48:17

I'll always remember when

My favorite school-related activity

More School Days

After school, I love to

_____

A school program that I will always remember

_____

_____

I'll never forget when I won

_____

_____

The thing I am most proud of

_____

_____

On winter breaks, I like to

_____

_____

On summer breaks, I like to

_____

_____

Attach school
photographs of
you and your friends,
projects, and programs

Let no one despise your youth, but be an example to the believers
in word, in conduct, in love, in spirit, in faith, in purity.

1 TIMOTHY 4:12 (NKJV)

I Praise You, God

The place where I go to worship

_____

_____

My favorite Sunday school teacher

_____

_____

My favorite hymn

_____

_____

The best lesson I've learned about God so far

_____

_____

_____

_____

Worshiping God is important because

_____

_____

_____

_____

"Let the little children come to me. Don't stop them.
The kingdom of God belongs to people who are like these little children."

MARK 10:14

When I really need to talk to God, I like to go to

_____

_____

_____

_____

In the News

The leader of our country is _____ .

The book that everyone is reading is _____ .

The most popular movie stars

_____

_____

Today's sports heroes

_____

_____

We get the news in our house by

_____

_____

Stories in the news

_____

_____

The big news in our family right now

_____

_____

_____

_____

"Don't let life discourage you; everyone who got
where he is had to begin where he was."
RICHARD L. EVANS

Merry Christmas to All!

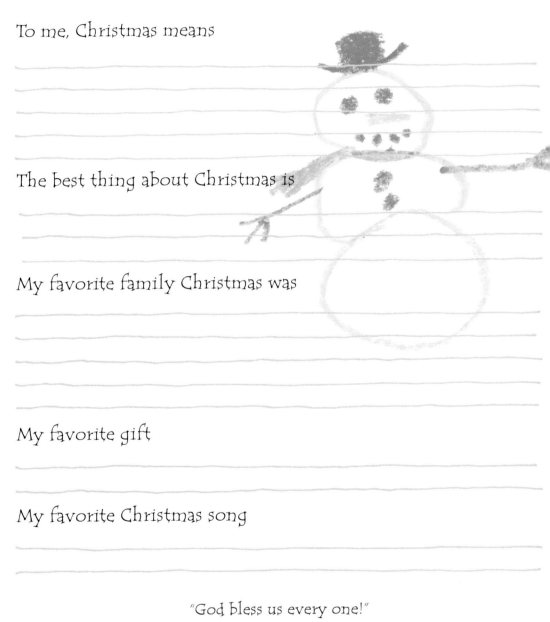

To me, Christmas means

The best thing about Christmas is

My favorite family Christmas was

My favorite gift

My favorite Christmas song

"God bless us every one!"
CHARLES DICKENS
A Christmas Carol

My favorite Christmas food

_____

_____

My favorite Christmas tradition

_____

_____

_____

_____

_____

_____

Happy Birthday to Me!

Birthdays are special in our home because

On my birthday, I

The best birthday present I ever received

My favorite kind of birthday cake

The child grew and became strong in spirit.

LUKE 1:80 (NKJV)

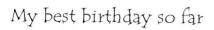

My best birthday so far

_____

_____

_____

_____

Other Special Days

At Easter, our family's tradition

In my family, the Fourth of July means

I think Halloween is fun because

For Thanksgiving, we always

Every year, on New Year's Day

Another special day we celebrate every year is

When I have my own family, a tradition I want to continue is

"Write it on your heart that every day is the best day in the year."
RALPH WALDO EMERSON

Hurray for Me!

Mom tells me I am the best at

_____

_____

_____

_____

Dad tells me I am the best at

_____

_____

_____

_____

_____

I think I am really good at

Mom tells everyone about the time that I

Dad tells everyone about the time that I

Special awards I have received

An award I would like to win

And they celebrated with great joy.

Just Mom and Me

Write about a special time you shared with your mom.

_I have no greater joy than to hear
that my children walk in truth._

3 JOHN 1:4 (NKJV)

Just Dad and Me

Write about a special time you shared with your dad.

_____
_____
_____
_____
_____
_____
_____
_____
_____
_____
_____
_____
_____
_____
_____
_____
_____
_____
_____
_____
_____
_____
_____

A wise son makes a glad father.

PROVERBS 10:1 (NKJV)

I Really Love You!

Attach pictures of
yourself with your
mom and dad,
family members,
and friends

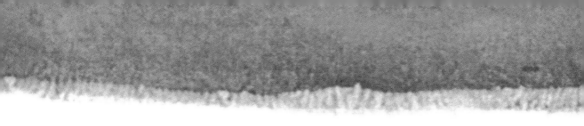

Attach pictures of
yourself with your
mom and dad,
family members,
and friends

I thank my God upon every remembrance of you.

Index of Paintings